THE INVASION OF THE
VAMPIRES

by Hermione Redshaw

Minneapolis, Minnesota

Credits

Images are courtesy of Shutterstock.com. With thanks to Getty Images, Thinkstock Photo, and iStockphoto. 2–3 – Anastacia-azzzya. 4–5 – Lario Tus, Dean Drobot. 6–7 – Virrage Images, Jakub Krechowicz. 8–9 – Independent birds, SB Arts Media. 10–11 – zef art, Ysbrand Cosijn. 12–13 – Ollyy. 14–15 – Nadezhda Bolotina, Adrian Stanica. 16–17 – PeskyMonkey, Claudio Gabriel Gonda. 18–19 – Mark Winfrey, Dm_Cherry. 20–21 – Elenfantasia, Ekaterina Bondaretc. 22–23 – Vera Petruk, Glevalex, Goji. 24–25 – Oleg Golovnev, 3doorsofsun. 26–27 – Maarina Vlasova, Yevhenii Orlov. 28–29 – Albina Tiplyashina, Kiselev Andrey Valerevich. 30 – Denis Makarenko, Anatoliy Karlyuk.

Bearport Publishing Company Product Development Team

President: Jen Jenson; Director of Product Development: Spencer Brinker; Managing Editor: Allison Juda; Associate Editor: Naomi Reich; Associate Editor: Tiana Tran; Senior Designer: Colin O'Dea; Associate Designer: Elena Klinkner; Associate Designer: Kayla Eggert; Product Development Specialist: Anita Stasson

Library of Congress Cataloging-in-Publication Data is available at www.loc.gov or upon request from the publisher.

ISBN: 979-8-88822-013-9 (hardcover)
ISBN: 979-8-88822-200-3 (paperback)
ISBN: 979-8-88822-328-4 (ebook)

© 2024 BookLife Publishing
This edition is published by arrangement with BookLife Publishing.

North American adaptations © 2024 Bearport Publishing Company. All rights reserved. No part of this publication may be reproduced in whole or in part, stored in any retrieval system, or transmitted in any form or by any means, electronic, mechanical, photocopying, recording, or otherwise, without written permission from the publisher.

For more information, write to Bearport Publishing, 5357 Penn Avenue South, Minneapolis, MN 55419.

CONTENTS

Are They Here? .4

Vampires in History 8

Spotting a Vampire 12

Places to Avoid 14

Hideout Hunting 18

Weapons and Tools 20

Defending Yourself 24

The Vampire Invasion 28

Surviving 30

Glossary 31

Index 32

Read More 32

Learn More Online 32

ARE THEY HERE?

Are there vampires living among us right now? Could they have been with us for thousands of years?

People say vampires are very clever. They try to make themselves hard to spot. But there are ways to tell . . .

Are people dying in strange ways? Do their bodies have bite marks on their necks? Were they **drained** of blood?

These clues could mean vampires are already here. And even worse, they want human blood!

Vampires are said to live mostly in the countryside. They sneak into towns in search of **prey**.

Vampires will try to make their attacks look like animals did them.

Vampires can hunt alone or as part of larger groups.

Some say vampires hunt two or three times a week. They can survive on animal blood if they need to.

But everyone knows a vampire's favorite meal is human blood!

VAMPIRES IN HISTORY

People have been telling stories about vampires for many years. Creatures that suck blood show up in **legends** from all over the world.

The creatures can look like ordinary men and women. However, they are neither dead nor alive!

Some people tell the story of Brahmaparusha (bra-ma-pa-ROOSH-a), a vampire-like creature in India.

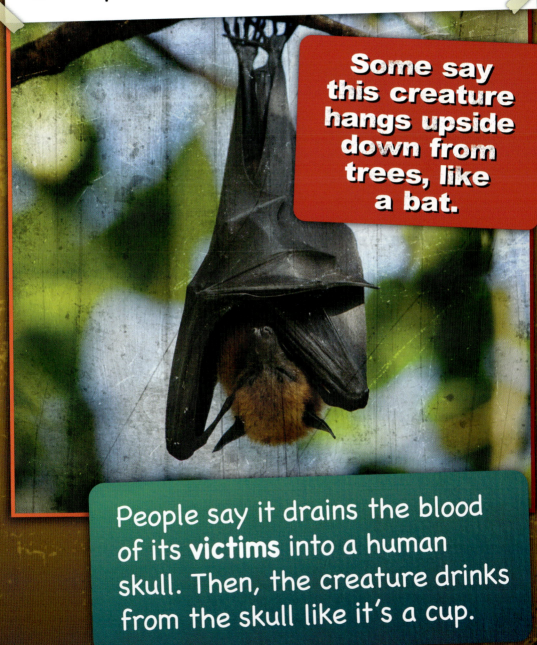

Some say this creature hangs upside down from trees, like a bat.

People say it drains the blood of its **victims** into a human skull. Then, the creature drinks from the skull like it's a cup.

Vrykolakas (vry-KAHL-a-kus) are evil creatures from Greek legends. They drink so much blood that their skin turns red.

Vrykolakas leave their graves to visit nearby homes. If you open your door when this creature knocks, you are sure to die.

One of the most famous vampire stories is of Count Dracula. He is very old. People say he can turn into a bat, a wolf, or a puff of smoke.

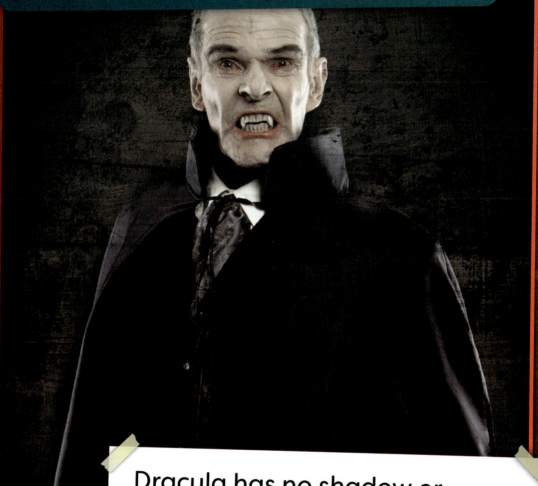

Dracula has no shadow or **reflection**. Like many vampires, he has two sharp **fangs**.

SPOTTING A VAMPIRE

How can you recognize a vampire? If there is an invasion, you will need this skill. Pay attention! There can be no mistakes.

CLOTHING

Some vampires still wear what they died in. Their clothes could look very old. You might even spot a vampire with a cape.

EYES

Vampire eyes glow red when they smell blood.

FANGS

Vampires have long, sharp fangs.

SKIN

Their skin is cold to the touch.

PLACES TO AVOID

The best way to avoid being attacked by vampires is to stay out of their way. Avoid places where vampires may live.

Be careful!

Vampires often move into **abandoned** castles. These places may still look empty after a bloodsucker has moved in.

Vampires can live anywhere in the world. Dracula and many other vampires come from a place called Transylvania.

Transylvania is an area in the country of Romania. People say hundreds of years ago, vampires built lots of castles high in the mountains there.

Some vampires live in graveyards. They stay in coffins deep underground to avoid the sun during the day.

Sunlight is harmful to vampires!

Be careful walking through graveyards in the dark! They are only safe to visit during the daytime.

Some vampires can turn into bats to travel at night. Then, they need to rest during the day.

It can be difficult to tell bats and vampires apart.

Some say vampires like to hang upside down in caves.

HIDEOUT HUNTING

To stay safe from vampires, you will need somewhere you can hide. You may need to be there for a long time.

Your **hideout** should be far away from castles, caves, and graveyards. The best hideouts get lots of sunlight.

Make sure your hideout has lots of food and water. Lock all the doors and windows.

Since vampires do not have reflections, you can trick them. Place a mirror near your entrance. You will be able to see if anyone visiting is secretly a vampire!

WEAPONS AND TOOLS

Vampires could turn up when you least expect them. You need to be prepared.

Having the right weapons could mean the difference between life and death. The best weapons are small, light, and can be easily hidden.

Vampire **slayers** throughout history have used garlic to keep the creatures away. No vampire will come anywhere near you if you stink of garlic.

Wear a string of garlic around your neck while you get other weapons ready.

Vampires do not like **sacred** objects, such as religious books or **symbols**.

Try carrying some of these around with you. They will protect you!

Vampires are not easy to kill. They are very strong and can heal quickly.

One way to kill a vampire is by putting a wooden stake through its heart. The stake can be made of any wood as long as it has a sharp, pointy end.

DEFENDING YOURSELF

Your hideout should be strong enough to keep you safe for a while. However, you may have to head outside when your supplies begin to run low.

Always go out in a group. Take plenty of wooden stakes with you.

Be sure to go out only during the daytime. Stay away from shadows.

Vampires that step into sunlight burst into flames and die.

25

You could try to trick a vampire into following you into sunlight.

If you pretend not to see a vampire, it might be fooled. You can also confuse or scare it with your sacred objects.

Most vampires are too clever to be tricked. Be prepared if you find yourself in the shadows.

Grab your wooden stake. You will need to get close enough to reach the vampire's heart.

THE VAMPIRE INVASION

If there is a vampire invasion, you will need to wait it out in your hideout. You can't go out and fight every vampire!

Sit back and settle down. It may be a long few months.

28

Vampires may become **desperate** toward the end of an invasion.

They may start running out of humans. This will make them very hungry. They might risk coming out in sunlight to attack.

SURVIVING

Don't worry. You have nothing to fear if you follow this guide.

Keep your doors locked. Be sure you have your garlic supply whenever you go outside. Most importantly, be back in your hideout before sunset!

GLOSSARY

abandoned empty or no longer in use

desperate feeling hopeless and doing things without thinking

drained emptied of liquid

fangs sharp, pointed teeth in the front of the mouth

hideout a safe place to hide from danger

legends stories that have been passed down from long ago but cannot be proven true

prey animals or people that are hunted for food

reflection an image that is seen in a mirror or on a shiny surface

sacred holy or religious

slayers killers

symbols objects or images that stand for something else

victims people who are attacked

Index

Brahmaparusha 9
Dracula 11, 15
garlic 21, 30
hideouts 18–19, 24, 28, 30

stakes 23–24, 27
supplies 24
vrykolakas 10
weapons 20–22, 26

Read More

Boutland, Craig. *Bloodthirsty Vampires (Unexplained).* Minneapolis: Lerner Publications, 2019.

Tyler, Madeline. *Vampire Investigators (Supernatural Science).* New York: Gareth Stevens Publishing, 2020.

Learn More Online

1. Go to **www.factsurfer.com** or scan the QR code below.
2. Enter "**Invasion of Vampires**" into the search box.
3. Click on the cover of this book to see a list of websites.